Hans Christian Andersen

The Little Mermaid

Retold by Jenny Dooley & Anthony Kerr

Stage 2 Pupil's Book

Express Publishing

Published by Express Publishing

Liberty House, New Greenham Park, Newbury,
Berkshire RG19 6HW
Tel.: (0044) 1635 817 363
Fax: (0044) 1635 817 463
e-mail: inquiries@expresspublishing.co.uk
http://www.expresspublishing.co.uk

First published 2002
Published in this edition 2007
Second impression 2008

Made in EU

ISBN 978-1-84325-800-1

CONTENTS

Who are the Merpeople?

There are some people
who live in the sea.
They do not walk
like you and me.

Chorus: They swim like fish.
They've got fishtails.
They dance with dolphins,
crabs and whales.

The merpeople make
homes of sand.
(There are some people
who live in the sea.)
And live in the ocean,
in Poseidon's land.
(They do not walk
like you and me.)

Repeat chorus

a king

a kingdom

swim

the sea

a mermaid

merpeople

a daughter

young

younger

youngest

There is a great kingdom,
under the sea,
where all the merpeople
live and swim free.
The King of the mermaids,
Poseidon the Great,
has six pretty daughters -
the youngest is eight.

7

golden hair

Once upon a time...

hear   tell

a grandmother

a land

far away

people

walk

Her name is Titania.
She's got golden hair.
She likes to hear stories
from Grandmother Fair.
She tells her stories
of a land far away
where people don't swim -
they 'walk', as they say.

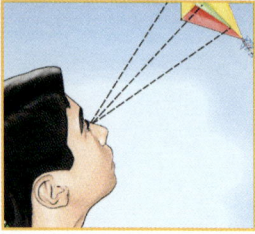

see

go

night

sleep

dream

10

"When can I see them?
Can we go now?"
"When you're sixteen, dear,
but not right now!"
So every night,
when it's time to sleep,
she dreams of this land
and then falls asleep.

11

surface

world

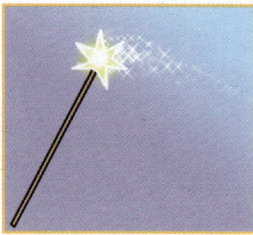

magic

a mountain

land

a bird

a bee

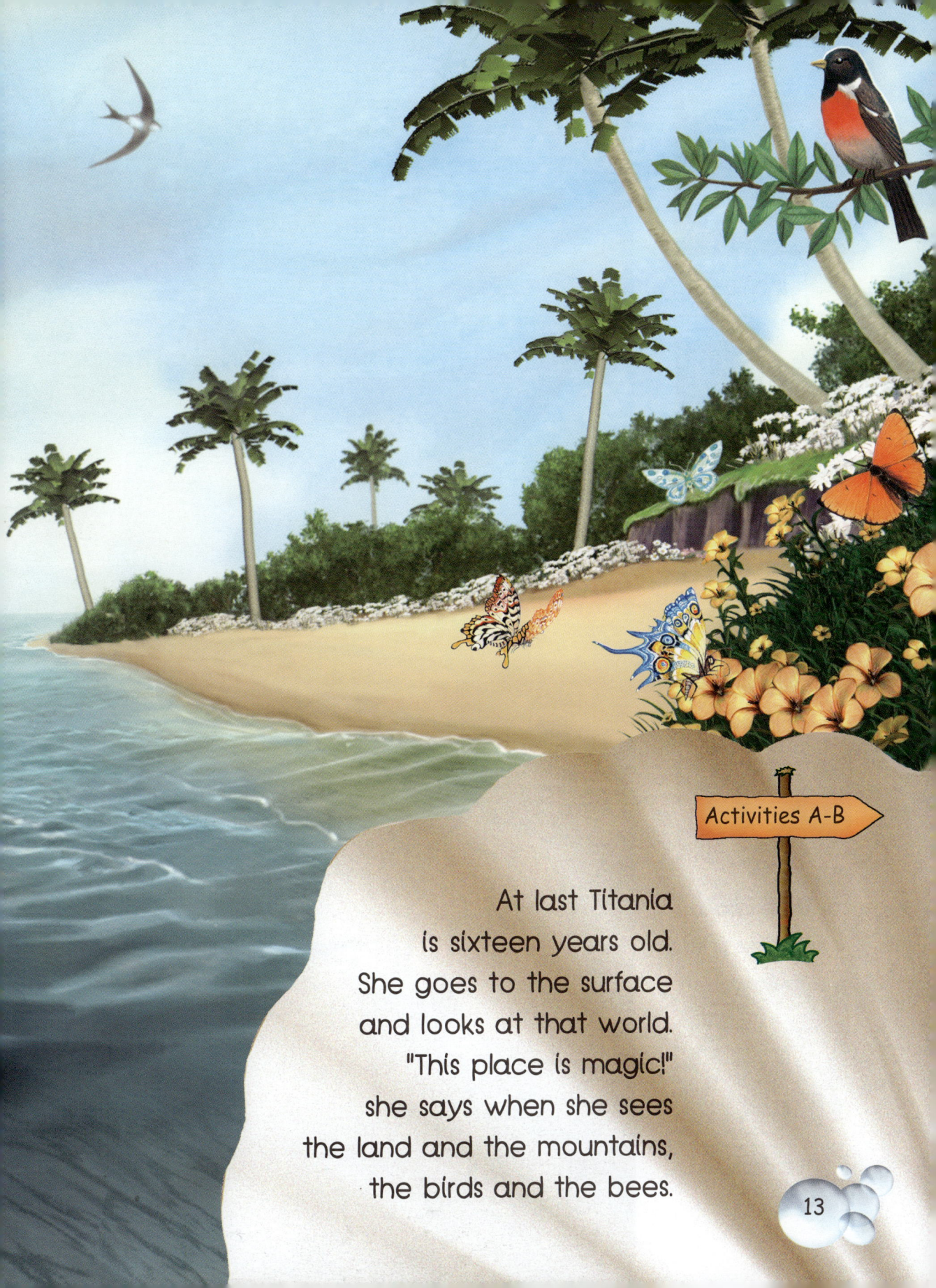

Activities A-B

At last Titania
is sixteen years old.
She goes to the surface
and looks at that world.
"This place is magic!"
she says when she sees
the land and the mountains,
the birds and the bees.

13

later

a trip

a big ship

a handsome prince

a deck

14

Some days later,
on a new trip,
the little mermaid
sees a big ship.
A handsome prince
is on deck that day.
Titania loves him
straight away.

15

the sun goes down

a strong wind

a wave

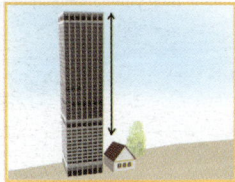

high

sink

drown

But when the sun
goes down that night
the wind gets strong,
the waves get high.
The big ship sinks.
The Prince falls down
into the water –
he's going to drown!

17

the shore

in danger

dive

cry

The mermaid takes him
to the shore.
He's not in danger
any more.
She looks at him
before she dives.
She wants to be with him,
and then she cries.

leave

an old witch

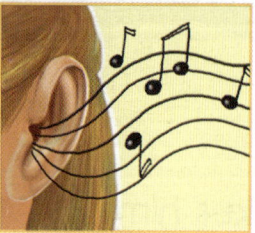

listen

Activities C-D

She quickly leaves
and goes to see
an old sea witch.
"Can you help me?"
The sea witch listens
and makes a plan.
"Of course, my dear!
You can marry a man!"

strong

human animal

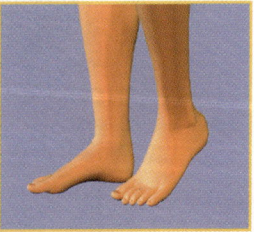

feet

"Give me your voice.
It's strong and sweet.
Then you can have
your human feet!"
"OK. Take it!
I do not care.
I just want him.
I think it's fair."

23

come back

die

turn into

foam

a husband   a wife

"But if you ever come back home, you're going to die and turn into foam. And if you can't be the Prince's wife, the price for that is your sweet life!"

drink

potion

"All right! I see!
But I want to try.
And if he doesn't love me,
then I must die!"
"Then drink this potion.
It's very strong.
And swim to the land
where you now belong."

What Can Titania Do?

Titania's sad.
She looks at the potion.
But how can she leave
her home in the ocean?

Chorus: It is very hard
to make the choice –
to leave her life
and lose her voice.

She thinks of her prince
and his beautiful land.
She must have her feet.
She must learn how to stand.

Repeat Chorus

She must have her feet.
She must learn how to stand.
To leave her life
and lose her voice.

an ocean

find

speak

Activities E-F

Titania drinks
the bitter potion
and says goodbye
to her home in the ocean.
She walks on land.
She's got her feet.
She finds the Prince,
but she can't speak.

look like

seek

"I think I know you.
But you can't speak.
You just look like
the girl I seek."
She wants to tell him
everything.
But poor Titania
can't say a thing.

33

take home

give clothes

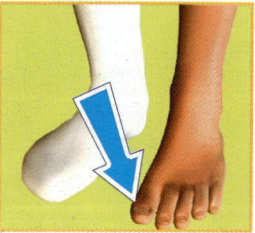

bare toes

happy   sad

new

old

He takes her home
and gives her clothes.
He feels sorry that
she's got bare toes.
Titania's happy
with her new life.
But the Prince is sad.
He wants a wife.

deep sea

a princess

share

a throne

He loves the mermaid
from the deep blue sea.
But he doesn't know
where she can be.
One day he brings
a new princess home
"I must marry **her**
and share my throne."

alone

Activity G

Titania now
is very sad!
He doesn't love her!
She feels so bad!
She walks to the sea
and cries alone.
She has no prince.
She has no home.

39

sisters

call

free

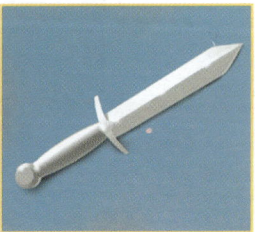

a silver knife

Her mermaid sisters
call from the sea.
"Kill the Prince
and you can be free!
Here you are, sister!
Take this silver knife!
Use it tonight
to end his life!"

a room

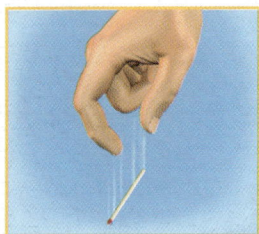

drop

wave

a beach

Titania cries
and goes to his room.
She cannot end
his life so soon!
She drops the knife
and waves goodbye.
She goes to the beach
where she must die.

jump into

save

float

above

Titania jumps
into the water.
King Poseidon
can't save his daughter.
But look! She floats
above her home!
She does not turn
into white foam!

a fairy

sky

fly

a heart

The little fairies
who can fly
take her away
into the sky.
"Because your heart
is kind and good,
you can stay with us,
in our fairy world!"

47

Activities H-K

So all ends well!
She does not die!
The mermaid lives,
up in the sky!

Wishes Can Go Wrong!

We sometimes ask for presents
our parents can't afford.
When we get something cheaper,
we say that we are bored.

Chorus: Be careful what you wish for –
it often turns out wrong!
Learn from the Little Mermaid and
listen to my song.

We should try to be happy
with everything we've got
and not want something different
or be someone we're not.

Repeat chorus (x2)

ACTIVITIES

Activities for pages 6-13

A Match the pictures to the words.

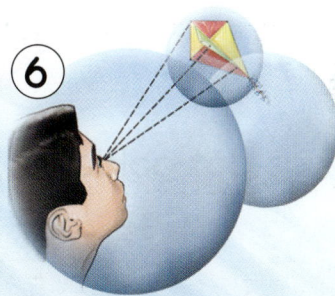

swim

hear

see

dream

go

walk

sleep

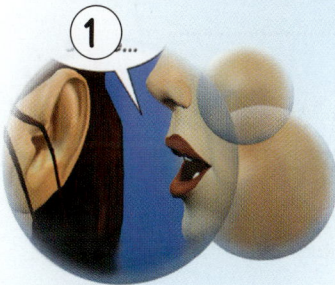

B Look at the pictures and write.

0 Your .....daughter..... is very beautiful!

1 What's your .... 's name?

2 Sheila has got golden ....

3 Merpeople live in the ....

4 Dolphins come to the .... for air.

5 Look at the .... in the tree!

6 My house is very .... away.

C Look at the pictures and write.

What am I?

I am on the ....sea.... . You can go on a ....

with me. You can sit on the .... and look at

the .... or watch the .... go

down at ....

What am I?

I'm a _ _ _ _ _ !

D Read the sentences and label the pictures.

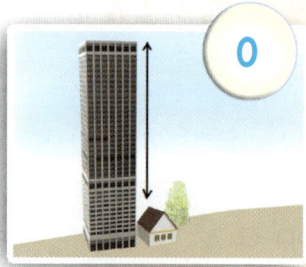

0

0 It's so high!

1 The Prince is very handsome!

2 The sun is going down.

3 The wind is so strong today!

4 Let's swim to the shore today!

E Look, read and (circle).

0

a sleep
b swim

1

a come back
b go

2

a die
b drown

3

a find
b turn into

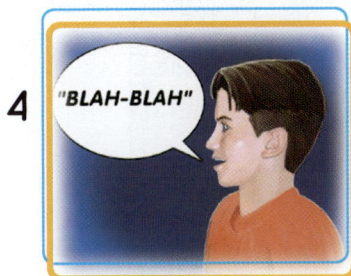

4

"BLAH-BLAH"

a speak
b listen

5

a cry
b leave

F Look and fill in the sentences.

0 This girl has got ....golden........ hair.

1 This is a .... prince.

2 This woman is in ....

3 This is the .... of the sea.

4 That is a big ....

5 This is an old ....

6 This man is very ....

7 This is a magic ....

G What are they doing? Look and write.

0

He _'s swimming_ .

1

They ....

2
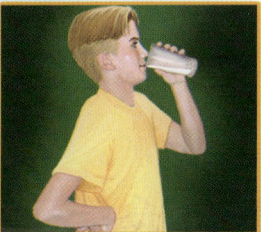

He ....

3

He ....
an answer to the mystery.

4

He .... the little
dog home.

5

She ....
her some clothes.

Activities for the whole story

H Look and write. Then find the words in the puzzle.

above ....

....

....

....

```
T C H E S P N C S X U S H O
C K U N A B O V E G S I H T
A T M O L F L A F F A S A D
I F A S O S D H E A R T P I
N W N A N E W S H A R E P H
S I L V E R K N I F E R Y I
K F S E A N I M A L C S F O
Y E H U S B A N D O U T L N
T R V Y J U T I F A I R Y N
K F M O R A M O R T R O O M
M E A N T W H A E T W N O U
L D N H L I S T E N I G F E
```

59

I   Do they rhyme? Look and write. Then, circle Yes or No.

0

(yes)   bee ....

no   free ....

4

yes   ....

no   ....

1

yes   ....

no   ....

5

yes   ....

no   ....

"BLAH-BLAH"

2

yes   ....

no   ....

6

yes   ....

no   ....

3

yes   ....

no   ....

7

yes   ....

no   ....

J Who says it? Write **T** for Titania, **P** for Prince, **O** for old sea witch or **F** for fairies.

0 "When can I see them?" .... T

1 "This place is magic." ....

2 "Give me your voice." ....

3 "OK. Take it! I do not care." ....

4 "You just look like the girl I seek." ....

5 "I must marry her and share my throne." ....

6 "Because your heart is kind and good, you can stay with us." ....

Titania

Prince

Sea Witch

Fairies

K Read the sentences and colour the picture.

Look at the little mermaid. She's in the blue sea. She's got golden hair. What is she doing? She's drinking a magic potion. It is green.

Now she's walking on the golden beach. She's wearing a yellow dress. And look at the Prince! He's got black hair. He's wearing black boots, blue trousers and a red shirt. He's talking to her.

▶ Now, let's act it out!

Actors: Titania   Sea witch   **Narrator:** The teacher, or a student,
Grandmother 3 Sisters   dressed as a fish.
Prince   Fairies

Song 1: Who are the Merpeople?

There are some people
who live in the sea.
They do not walk
like you and me.

Chorus: They swim like fish.
They've got fishtails.
They dance with dolphins,
crabs and whales.

The merpeople make
homes of sand.
(There are some people
who live in the sea.)
And live in the ocean,
in Poseidon's land.
(They do not walk
like you and me.)

Repeat chorus

Scene 1

Narrator: There is a great kingdom,
under the sea,
where all the merpeople
live and swim free.

Narrator:	The King of the mermaids, Poseidon the Great, has six pretty daughters – the youngest is eight.
	Her name is Titania. She's got golden hair. She likes to hear stories from Grandmother Fair.
	She tells her stories of a land far away, where people don't swim – they 'walk', as they say.
Titania:	When can I see them? Can we go now?
Grand-mother:	When you're sixteen, dear, but not right now!
Narrator:	So every night, when it's time to sleep, she dreams of this land and then falls asleep.
	At last Titania is sixteen years old. She goes to the surface and looks at that world.
Titania:	This place is magic!
Narrator:	She says when she sees the land and the mountains, the birds and the bees.
	Some days later on a new trip, the little mermaid sees a big ship.

Narrator: A handsome prince
is on deck that day.
Titania loves him
straight away.

But when the sun
goes down that night,
the wind gets strong,
the waves get high.

The big ship sinks.
The Prince falls down
into the water –
he's going to drown!

The mermaid takes him
to the shore.
He's not in danger
any more.

She looks at him
before she dives.
She wants to be with him,
and then she cries.

She quickly leaves
and goes to see
an old sea witch.

Titania: Can you help me?

Narrator: The sea witch listens
and makes a plan.

Sea Witch: Of course, my dear!
You can marry a man!
Give me your voice.
It's strong and sweet.
Then you can have
your human feet!

Titania: OK. Take it!
I do not care.
I just want him
I think it's fair.

Sea Witch: But if you ever
come back home,
you're going to die
and turn into foam.

And if you can't be
the Prince's wife,
the price for that
is your sweet life.

Titania: All right! I see!
But I want to try.
And if he doesn't love me,
then I must die!

Sea Witch: Then drink this potion.
It's very strong.
And swim to the land
where you now belong.

Song 2: What Can Titania Do?

Titania's sad.
She looks at the potion.
But how can she leave
Her home in the ocean?

Chorus: It is very hard
to make the choice -
to leave her life
and lose her voice.

Word List

The words in colour are presented in the picture dictionary in the main story.

above
all ends well
all right
alone
animal
any more
at last
bad
bare
beach
bee
belong (belonged)
big
bird
bitter
blue
bring (brought)
call (called)
care (cared)
clothes
come back (came back)
cry (cried)
daughter
day
dear
deck
deep

die (died)
dive (dived)
dream (dreamt)
drink (drank)
drop (dropped)
drown (drowned)
end
ever
every
everything
fair
fairy
fall asleep (fell asleep)
fall down (fell down)
far away
feel (felt)
feet (foot-feet)
find (found)
float (floated)
fly (flew)
foam
free
get (got)
girl
give (gave)
go (went)
go down (went down)

golden hair
good
goodbye
grandmother
great
handsome
happy
have got (had got)
hear (heard)
heart
help (helped)
here
high
home
human
husband
in danger
jump into (jumped into)
just
kill (killed)
kind
king
kingdom
knife (knives)
know (knew)
land (country)
land (ground)

71

Word List

later

leave (left)

life (lives)

like (liked)

listen (listened)

little

live (lived)

look at (looked at)

look like (looked like)

love (loved)

magic

make (made)

man (men)

marry (married)

mermaid

merpeople

mountain

name

new

night

now

ocean

of course

old

people (person-people)

place

plan

poor

potion

pretty

price

prince

princess

quickly

right now

room

sad

save (saved)

say (said)

sea

see (saw)

see (understand)

seek (sought)

share (shared)

ship

shore

silver

sink (sank)

sister

sky

sleep (slept)

soon

sorry

speak (spoke)

stay (stayed)

story

straight away

strong

sun

surface

sweet

swim

take (took)

take sb away

tell (told)

then

thing

think (thought)

throne

time

toe

tonight

trip

try (tried)

turn into (turned into)

under

use (used)

voice

walk (walked)

want (wanted)

water

wave (n)

wave (waved)

white

wife (wives)

wind

witch

world

young-younger-youngest